The Honorable Alternative:

A Conservative Case for Johnson/Weld in 2016

Brian Gongol

This publication is intended to provide accurate and authoritative information on the topics presented, but is not intended as any form of legal, accounting, or other professional advice. No relationship is established between the author or publisher and any other party in the exchange of this publication. The subject matter described is subject to change and any recommendations or advice pertaining thereto is similarly subject to change without notice.

First edition, September 2016

Index

The Honorable Alternative

America:
We Can Do Better

Americans have faced many challenging elections in the past – contests that revealed regional strife, economic divisions, and unsavory elements of the national character.

Americans have also persisted through times of terrible leadership. **Not every President is a George Washington, an Abraham Lincoln, or a Teddy Roosevelt.** Some have been substantially incompetent or even recklessly close to criminal.

It is a sign of our strength as a nation that we have peacefully persisted through our low times. But we also should never let down our guard and permit complacency to win. We are at a point of weakness in our national character today: We face an election in which the two major parties have nominated candidates who are abnormally bad.

The Democratic Party has nominated former Secretary of State Hillary Clinton. She possesses a resume of service in the United States Senate and in the State Department. She has never led as an elected executive (like a governor or a big-city mayor), so we have never had the opportunity to see how she performs in a role analogous to the Presidency.

We do know that she has, on several prominent occasions, behaved as though she is above the law. The most contemporary example, perhaps, is in her deliberate choice to set up a personal e-mail system on which to conduct government business while serving as Secretary of State. While she argues that it was merely a matter of convenience for herself, the very act itself suggests that **she simply does not behave as though she is subject to the law in the same way that it applies to ordinary people.**

As a Yale-educated lawyer[1], a former First Lady of the State of Arkansas and of the United States, and a former United States Senator with a top-secret security clearance[2], she simply cannot make any reasonable case that she didn't understand the ramifications for security or compliance with open-records laws that would have come with conducting business on a personal, "home-brew" e-mail system.

* * *

On the other hand, the Republican Party has nominated Donald Trump. His megalomaniacal self-absorption, inability to comprehend the fundamentals of Constitutional law, and careless incitement of violence and racism are so far outside the normal bounds of civilized behavior that he is a unique hazard to the office of the Presidency itself.

For all of the many things that make Hillary Clinton a bad choice for the office, Donald Trump has shown himself to be demonstrably worse.

Trump is a hazard not because of his own powers – he isn't very bright and shows no real interest in doing the job of President. Whatever power is vested with the President himself would likely find itself mostly abdicated or executed with "low energy", as Trump himself so famously panned his Republican rival, Jeb Bush.

Not because of what he could do to destroy the government – the Constitution was specifically designed to be stronger than any one individual, and whatever our other disagreements on policies, most Americans will rise to the defense of the separation of powers. Fortunately, we have a strong Speaker of the House and a strong Chief Justice, both of whom can be expected to do what is right and necessary to defend the system of government itself.

No, the existential threat Donald Trump poses is social and cultural instead. It's one thing to let the inmates run the asylum when you're in a middle-school classroom full of hormonal teenagers. In a place like

---

1   HillaryClinton.com: https://www.hillaryclinton.com/about/hillary/
2   USA Today: http://www.usatoday.com/story/news/politics/2016/07/05/hillary-clinton-fbi-investigation-security-clearance/86709410/

that, the class clown can hijack control from a weak-willed teacher and often will do so. But the Oval Office is no such place. **The dignity of the Oval Office is like a bonsai tree: It grows very slowly, requires extremely careful cultivation, and doesn't recover quickly from damage.**

Presidents of both parties have done grave harm to the dignity of the office already – the Nixon tapes demonstrate just what harm comes from a President who speaks his biased, paranoid, unfiltered mind. The sex scandals of Bill Clinton's time put on display the harm that comes when a President puts his literal self-gratification above the seriousness of the office.

* * *

In the case of Donald Trump, we face an unwise, unrestrained, endlessly self-gratifying man-child. He represents the worst selfishness of Bill Clinton, the worst megalomania of Richard Nixon, and the most loathsome appeals to corruption and self-aggrandizement seen since the Harding administration. The man won voters in the primary process specifically by parading his experience "buying" elected officials.

This is the damage we face: An Oval Office not just tarnished, but permanently knocked off the pedestal of respect upon which it must stand if we are to be a superpower.

And there is no escaping the meaning of this void: **A world without a respected superpower will give way to a world filled with regional powers and unstable superpowers-in-waiting.** Russia has demonstrated what it is willing to do in and around Europe to make a show of strength – invading Ukraine, threatening the Baltic States, and invading the airspace of NATO nations. China has such little regard for the present world order that it is constructing artificial islands in the South China Sea, just to expand its territorial claims and infringe on the well-being of smaller nations.

And where no such powers are ascendant, things are often even worse – Somalia, Libya, and Yemen are just three failed states in Africa and the Middle East, among more than a dozen that could be called "highly fragile"[3]. Venezuela – a nation just 500 miles from Puerto Rico, or perhaps an hour's flight time by fighter or bomber jet – is on the brink of collapse at any moment, here in our own hemisphere.

You may look at these examples of pending disaster and blame our response, in part, on the weakness of the Obama Administration. And you may even be right about that. Over the last eight years, we have failed to project strength on the world stage and that may have emboldened our rivals while failing to stiffen the backbones of our allies.

But **strength is not effectively projected by empty bombast**, and that is all that Donald Trump supplies. He is, in the old Texas phrase, all hat and no cattle. This is a man who thinks strength is projected by demeaning United States Senators of both parties (pejoratively dismissing "Little" Marco Rubio, "Lyin'" Ted Cruz, and "Pocahantas" Elizabeth Warren).

It is one thing to disagree or to contest with the other branches of government – but the United States Senate also bears the responsibility to advise and consent on all matters of foreign policy [Article II, Section 2], and it is Congress alone that is authorized to declare war [Article I, Section 8].

Donald Trump's fundamental failure to respect the people charged with checking the power of the Presidency makes him a demagogue-in-waiting. His concept of Presidential power is like his concept of class – he wants the shine but doesn't have the intellect or self-discipline to do the polishing. **In the same way that the buildings that bear his name often don't actually belong to him, he wants glory but not responsibility.**

* * *

---

3   Foreign Policy, "Fragile States Index": http://foreignpolicy.com/fragile-states-index-2016-brexit-syria-refugee-europe-anti-migrant-boko-haram/

It doesn't have to be like this.

Elected officials – whatever their party or ideology – should be expected to demonstrate three simple but irreplaceable characteristics: Curiosity, competence, and humility.

The President of the United States doesn't face routine problems. The real problems that reach the President are almost exclusively original – they haven't happened to anyone before. Problems that have easy answers get resolved before they reach the President's desk.

That makes it essential – literally mandatory...not optional in any way – that the President possess a high level of curiosity. **An uncurious person cannot perform the duties of President in any satisfactory way.**

Competence should speak for itself. Competence to hold the highest executive office in the land can be demonstrated in several ways, but the way most likely to give voters a reasonable evaluation is that the candidate should have held a substantial elected executive office in the past – preferably governor of a state, or mayor of a very large city (since there are metropolitan governors who oversee administrations larger than those of some small states).

Previous elected-executive experience can be used to show whether a person is capable of executing the laws passed by others (a legislature or a large city council) and doing so in a competent and faithful manner, even when the executive doesn't agree with those laws. A person could conceivably pass through a term in meaningful elected-executive office without facing any real trials, but it's not very common. The experience of a governor or a major metropolitan mayor almost always gives the public some kind of window into the individual's competence as a leader under difficult conditions – as well as his or her ability to put capable people into important positions of responsibility. **Until we have such a thing as an Oval Office simulator, the best available test of a person's competence to be President is their prior performance as an elected executive.**

Humility may sound like a joke (what person could be humble while running for the highest office in the land?), but it may be the most valuable characteristic of all. There is a saying that suggests that a business executive should want their employees to be honest, smart, and motivated – in that order. Without honesty, an employer definitely doesn't want someone with the other two. In the case of an elected officer of government, we want them to be curious and competent – but we cannot give them great power without great humility. **Politicians who lack humility are at grave risk of trying to do things that they shouldn't and embarking on schemes that are destined to fail.** They are dangerous precisely because they don't acknowledge that they could be wrong.

* * *

Ordinarily, the candidates of the two major parties are the only ones worth consideration. America's first-past-the-post electoral system and our dedication to the principle of "one person, one vote" have the effect of leading naturally to a two-party system – a duopoly, if you will – not because of any systemic corruption or because the system is "rigged", but because a two-party system is the only outcome that remains stable in the long run[4].

However...in the short run, sometimes things can become profoundly unstable. The two-party system in America depends upon the parties' ability to form coalitions among different interest groups before the election (during the primary/nomination process), and for those coalitions to show up in large numbers on election day.

When forces big enough to tear apart those coalitions come into the picture, the two-party system can become unstable – potentially unstable enough to permit the rise of alternative parties. **For the first time in decades, the two-party system is just that unstable.** This is an unusual condition; normally, math would reset the two-party

---

4   If you are truly interested in this question, read the book <u>Why Flip a Coin?</u>, by H.W. Lewis. It explains in detail why no system of voting is perfect and why people everywhere are frustrated by their politicians as a result of this imperfection.

duopoly and make third-party votes ineffective as a means of achieving either results or meaningful protest. Perhaps not in 2016.

* * *

There are two reasons to take seriously the third-party option in 2016. First, there is a substantial population that is utterly disaffected with the two options. Independents are just a little shy of a majority of the population in the Gallup Poll[5]. And, perhaps just as important, a historically reliable wing of the Republican Party coalition (variously described as "Main Street", "pro-business", or even "moderate" Republicans) are being publicly rejected and repelled by the Republican candidate. These facts together signal very high instability in the traditional electoral coalitions.

The second reason is that, extraordinarily, there is a third-party ticket with a credible claim to participate in the race. The Libertarian Party has taken the extraordinary step of nominating two former governors as their ticket in 2016: Two-term New Mexico Governor Gary Johnson, and two-term Massachusetts Governor William Weld. Both governors were elected as Republicans to serve in heavily Democratic-leaning states, and both were re-elected to their second terms with larger margins of victory than in their first.

This is very unusual behavior on the part of the Libertarian Party, which has historically been driven more by ideological purity than by practical expectations of results. The libertarianism of Johnson and Weld isn't for the purists – but it is exceptionally close to what might be called the libertarian core of the American electorate: Fiscally conservative but socially tolerant.

The United States is widely viewed as a center-right nation; in general, we are slow to embrace change. But we also celebrate a national character that tends to resist government interference in the lives of individuals.

---

5   Gallup, "Party Affiliation": http://www.gallup.com/poll/15370/party-affiliation.aspx

This individualist streak aligns fairly well with a centrist version of libertarianism: One that seeks primarily to reduce the scale and scope of government wherever doing so won't be too disruptive to the lives of ordinary Americans, while generally adopting a live-and-let-live philosophy of personal tolerance.

Is that the libertarianism of the most passionate Libertarian Party activists? Probably not. But it is one that reflects the beliefs of a large and (temporarily?) homeless wing of the Republican Party, as well as of a large share of independent voters.

Altogether, the conditions are unusually good – really, possibly unique in modern times – for a credible third-party campaign for the White House.

Limited Government
Matters Most

Many Americans share a common concern about the influence of money in politics. In the 2016 race, we have heard Donald Trump brag about his use of campaign contributions to buy influence[6] and we have seen Hillary Clinton's campaign get serious (and well-deserved) scrutiny over whether donations to the Clinton Foundation may have influenced her work at the State Department[7].

While there are lots of opinions on whether and how to try to control the influence of money on politics, the fact is that the money in politics is chasing power, and the more power government has, the more incentive outsiders will have to try to influence that power. Government may be necessary, but it also shouldn't be let out of control. **A free society must put limits on its government.**

Perhaps the most potent symbol of limited government and what it should best be doing is the interstate highway system. The government has provided a fundamental and basic infrastructure that permits and enhances free movement and commerce among the states. By supplying a modern surface-transportation infrastructure, government is acting to facilitate commerce and free movement.

And while the government funds the roadways, it very rarely does the actual construction. The government sets standards, and collectively we pay for roadways we all use in common, but private contractors are ordinarily the ones to actually perform the construction. And once that

---

6   Trump boasted openly about this in a debate in August 2015. See ABC News, "Donald Trump's Surprisingly Honest Lessons About Big Money in Politics": http://abcnews.go.com/Politics/donald-trumps-surprisingly-honest-lessons-big-money-politics/story?id=32993736

7   Criticism on this matter came from partisan and neutral sources alike. The Washington Post, for example, covered the story under an August 2016 headline of "Emails Reveal How Foundation Donors Got Access to Clinton and Her Close Aides at State Dept.": https://www.washingtonpost.com/politics/emails-reveal-how-foundation-donors-got-access-to-clinton-and-her-close-aides-at-state-dept/2016/08/22/345b5200-6882-11e6-8225-fbb8a6fc65bc_story.html

construction is complete, individuals and firms are free to use those roadways within the bounds of limited rules and regulations. **Government rules paint the lines to separate the lanes, but no agent of government drives your car for you.** You remain free to make the choices about where to go, when to use it, and what to drive.

This, ultimately, is what government is supposed to do. It is mainly supposed to act as a referee to keep us from harming one another. In his confirmation hearing, Supreme Court Chief Justice John Roberts said, "I will remember that it's my job to call balls and strikes, and not to pitch or bat."[8] What is true for the Supreme Court is broadly true for the government at large. The philosophy of **free people making free choices under the rule of law** is hardly anything radical in America – it's what the nation was founded upon.

Thus it is disturbing to find ourselves in the current predicament.

On the left, the Bernie Sanders movement has consciously used the word "revolution" with a mix of excitement and anticipation. **"Revolution" is a word that ought to be used only with great caution** – Sanders seems not to have meant it in the metaphorical sense (as in, "Reagan Revolution"), but rather in something much closer to literal revolution. His post-candidacy organization even took the name "Our Revolution".

This left-wing "revolution" seeks to make too many things into birthrights: Free college tuition may be the hallmark[9], but the left wing shows no sign of stopping at that. And for everything they promise to give away for "free", someone has to pay. The left wing's approach to this has been to demonize profits and wealth, often in radical language rarely heard in American politics. Had Senator Sanders been speaking of a racial, religious, or ethnic group the way he spoke in his campaign about "the billionaires", it would have been hate speech.

---

8   Administrative Office of the U.S. Courts: http://www.uscourts.gov/educational-resources/educational-activities/chief-justice-roberts-statement-nomination-process

9   Sen. Sanders vigorously promoted his free-tuition promises on the stump and in an editorial published in the Washington Post: https://www.washingtonpost.com/opinions/bernie-sanders-america-needs-free-college-now/2015/10/22/a3d05512-7685-11e5-bc80-9091021aeb69_story.html?tid=a_inl&utm_term=.b4384c9ea780

On the right, a very old version of isolationist populism has overcome lots of people who fear "the Other", whatever that "other" may be. Promises of border walls are just the beginning. When Donald Trump says things like "America first", he's using the equivalent of a dog whistle to stoke nationalism and instigate racism. And there has been a strong and disconcerting response from people who call themselves the "alt-right" – the latest reincarnation of neo-Nazism and white-supremacist belief.

Make no mistake about it: Donald Trump has, consciously or not, taken these loathsome messages and amplified them. It has happened most visibly on his Twitter account, where he recycled, retweeted, or otherwise amplified white supremacist messages in January[10], February[11], April[12], and July 2016[13] alone. Moreover, after abundant criticism and ample time to recant, he has left all of the messages in place. When a normal, reasonable person makes a mistake, he or she admits the error and seeks to correct it. **Trump has made no such effort to correct these obvious failures in judgment**, despite widespread criticism. He obstinately refuses to acknowledge his bad choices or to correct his ways. Instead, he has doubled-down on policies like anti-immigration proposals and returned over and over to the same rhetoric that hasn't fit with America's vision of itself in many decades.

Neither of these movements – far-left or far-right – fits with the philosophy of a free country under the rule of law. Neither the confiscation of profits nor the exclusion of immigrants and refugees (particularly because of the color of their skin or their professions of religious belief) is in keeping with the great American tradition.

---

10 Trump re-tweeted a picture from an account with the name "White Genocide" on January 22, 2016: https://twitter.com/realDonaldTrump/status/690562515500032000

11 Politico noted that Trump thanked a white supremacist in a tweet on February 27, 2016: http://www.politico.com/blogs/2016-gop-primary-live-updates-and-results/2016/02/donald-trump-white-supremacist-retweet-219915

12 The Hill noted Trump's re-tweet of a message from a Dutch white supremacist and pointed out that he had amplified the same person's posts on at least five other occasions: http://thehill.com/blogs/ballot-box/gop-primaries/276919-trump-retweets-another-apparent-white-supremacist

13 Long after receiving criticism for his other Twitter indiscretions, Trump recycled a message with obvious anti-Semitic imagery: http://www.nbcnews.com/politics/2016-election/donald-trump-s-star-david-tweet-about-hillary-clinton-posted-n603161

This is serious stuff, and it's not enough to just roll over and go along to get along. These are not trivial deviations on either side.

As we have adopted it in the modern era, the American Way acknowledges a role for government but seeks always to roll it back to the point where it does no more than what it must do. **One might say we want only as much government as we really need, but no more than that.** Donald Trump has made not one serious suggestion that he wants to reduce the role of government – and, regrettably, neither has Hillary Clinton.

The only Presidential ticket seriously advocating restraint on government spending, activity, or intervention in the lives of the American people is Gary Johnson and William Weld. They have the right rhetoric on the matter:

> *"By 2017, the national debt will be $20 TRILLION. That is not just obscene, it is unsustainable – and arguably the single greatest threat to our national security."[14]*

Moreover, each has a specific track record of budgetary discipline. As governors, both Johnson and Weld were known for aggressively cutting spending and seeking to reduce the scale of government[15]. They can say without reservation, "Don't just take my word for it" – they behaved exactly as promised. **Johnson and Weld have real credibility as small-government leaders.** There is no better time to start getting government under control than the present – and that has always been true.

Consider this rule of thumb for government: **Never assume powers that you don't want your opponents to have when it's their turn to run the show.** If you don't like the idea of an uncontrolled egomaniac getting the levers of government, if you want to put the brakes on cronyism, or if you want to ensure that future politicians don't have

---

14 JohnsonWeld.com: https://www.johnsonweld.com/wasteful_spending
15 The Cato Institute, an aggressively small-government think tank, has noted that it had credited both governors with reducing government in their states and balancing budgets: http://www.cato.org/blog/cato-fiscal-grades-gary-johnson-william-weld

more power than you would entrust to your opponents, then for this election there is a credible, experienced, and honorable option on the ballot: Gary Johnson and William Weld.

Law and Order:
A Peaceful Nation at Home

Donald Trump has sought to inject the theme of "law and order" into the 2016 campaign. He appears to hope that creating a sense of fear about crime will do for him what it did for Richard Nixon in 1968[16], but it flies in the face of the facts: While a handful of places have become measurably more violent in recent years (Chicago is probably the most prominent example), the nation's overall rate of violent crime is lower than it was in Nixon's era[17].

Crime rates have fallen over the past five years[18], and despite year-to-year fluctuations, there is really no evidence at all to support a renewed fear of crime. Some stories certainly have become more prominent because they are easy to share via social media, and specific crimes like the murder of police officers in Dallas have been put in the spotlight. **These circumstances may be elevating the perception that crime is rampant – but the facts do not support that conclusion.**

Economic prosperity, healthy civic institutions, and a widespread respect for the law (and for the rights of others) all contribute to safer streets and a lower rate of crime – but they don't have the same gut-level emotional appeal as promises to "get tough on crime". That's too bad, because our focus really ought to be on those conditions that create a foundation for a peaceful, law-abiding nation.

We must look to those systemic factors if we really want public security. A focus on locking up criminals is too little, too late. It is much better to keep people out of trouble in the first place, and to rehabilitate as many as possible of those who end up inside the criminal justice system so that they don't come back. Repeat offenders should be taken as a

16 Politico did a thorough report on this effort to recycle 50-year-old themes in a July 2016 article: http://www.politico.com/magazine/story/2016/07/donald-trump-law-and-order-richard-nixon-crime-race-214066
17 Federation of American Scientists, "Is Violent Crime in the United States Increasing?": https://www.fas.org/sgp/crs/misc/R44259.pdf
18 FBI, "Preliminary Uniform Crime Report 2015": https://ucr.fbi.gov/crime-in-the-u.s/2015/preliminary-semiannual-uniform-crime-report-januaryjune-2015/tables/table-3

symptom of a malfunctioning system: Anyone who commits a serious crime after spending time in prison for a previous crime is a deadweight cost to taxpayers – and a threat to the public that failed to "correct" their behavior the first time through the system.

Unfortunately, though, the major-party candidates in 2016 are terrible messengers for a safer, more law-abiding society. Hillary Clinton has too often behaved as though she is above the law, while Donald Trump's words suggest he doesn't fully understand that the law exists[19]. While Clinton seems to be perpetually shrouded in a fog of suspicious behavior, Trump plainly cannot be taken seriously as a law-abiding citizen, much less as the individual responsible at the highest level for carrying out the law.

Donald Trump cannot be excused for his willful ignorance of the law and cannot be trusted to enforce it. This is the man who has joked that his popularity makes him untouchable ("I could stand in the middle of 5th Avenue and shoot somebody and I wouldn't lose voters"[20]), thinks that the First Amendment should take a back seat to his own interests ("I'm going to open up our libel laws so when they write purposely negative and horrible and false articles, we can sue them and win lots of money"[21]), and made an off-color remark about assassination ("If she gets to pick her judges, nothing you can do, folks...Although the Second Amendment people – maybe there is, I don't know"[22]). These aren't mere accidents or slips of the tongue: They reveal his total absence of respect for the rule of law.

Their shortcomings in this important regard only serve to elevate the importance of injecting reasonable people into the debate – literally, on the stage at the debates, and ultimately (if possible) on election day

---

19   See, for instance, his absurd claims about "loosening" libel laws, his enthusiasm for bankruptcy filings as a "tool" for conducting business, or his casual and careless incitements to violence when speaking in front of large crowds. He fails to show the common respect for the law that we expect from any other reasonable adult, and he does it on a massive scale.
20   CNN, "Trump: I Could 'Shoot Somebody and I wouldn't Lose Voters'": http://www.cnn.com/2016/01/23/politics/donald-trump-shoot-somebody-support/
21   Politico, "Donald Trump: We're Going to 'Open Up' Libel Laws": http://www.politico.com/blogs/on-media/2016/02/donald-trump-libel-laws-219866
22   New York Times, "Donald Trump Suggests 'Second Amendment People' Could Act Against Hillary Clinton": http://www.nytimes.com/2016/08/10/us/politics/donald-trump-hillary-clinton.html?_r=0

itself. In the modern era, we have treated the President as the legislator-in-chief. But a plain reading of the Constitution should be all the reminder any of us should need that the President of the United States is responsible for executing the laws that are passed by Congress. Article I establishes the legislative branch; Article II establishes the executive. The former initiates the laws, and the latter puts them into force.

Or, to take the words from the Constitution itself: **The President "shall take Care that the Laws be faithfully executed"**[23]. This is not a voluntary condition of the job. It is an explicit duty of the office.

If you want to see a duty like this conducted well, then you should look first to those who have experience doing the same type of job. The people best-suited to execute the law on a national scale are those who have had similar experience on the second-largest scale: State governors. The experience itself is indispensable, but it also tends to help temper their enthusiasm for the power of the government to do more than it should. People with experience as governors gain first-hand experience in the consequences of bad laws, badly-chosen administrators of the law, and the unintended consequences that follow from the law. To govern, in short, ought to be an exercise in humility about just how much to expect from the law.

Taking a look at our crime statistics with a dose of humility gives one an appreciation for the fact we, as a country, are doing something wrong.

Our country currently has a prison population of 2.2 million people[24], according to the US Department of Justice Bureau of Justice Statistics. **That makes our prison population the size of San Francisco, Milwaukee, and Nashville**[25]**, combined.** Another 4.7 million Americans are on parole or probation.

---

23   Article II, Section 3: http://www.archives.gov/exhibits/charters/constitution_transcript.html
24   US Department of Justice, "Correctional Populations in the United States, 2014", revised January 21, 2016: http://www.bjs.gov/content/pub/pdf/cpus14.pdf
25   The Census Bureau reports population estimates for 2015 of 864,816 for San Francisco, 682,545 for Denver, and 654,610 for Nashville: http://factfinder.census.gov/faces/tableservices/jsf/pages/productview.xhtml?src=bkmk

If you think that that is a useful and productive way for us to put our people to work, then there's really not much more to be gained from reading this chapter.

But if you are willing to step back and objectively view the big picture, the concept of having nearly 7 million Americans actively under the watch of the correctional system looks like a giant waste of human productivity and potential.

Only a fraction of those people are truly sociopathic and really need to be warehoused in order to keep the rest of us safe. If the psychologists are right, no more than about one out of every 100 people is wired to be truly anti-social[26].

The remainder should otherwise be considered normal people who made bad decisions, and are best treated with rehabilitation and reform rather than permanent imprisonment. It's bad enough that people commit crimes; we make the situation far worse for ourselves if we don't take steps to make sure most of them leave the justice system as better people than when they entered. Imprisonment has far-reaching consequences for families and other innocent parties, too. We need to do something to reform our criminal agenda.

One of the most important factors involved is nonviolent drug crime. The people who are caught up in our prison system as a result of nonviolent drug offenses are people who require treatment and attention, generally in a non-prison setting. Let's reserve our limited prison capacity for protecting other people who need protection from the true sociopaths among us. For the rest, reform and rehabilitation is a far more sensible option.

If you instinctively object to anything about the Libertarian Party platform, it is probably the party's position on drug legalization. But, putting aside whether any drugs ought to be legalized or

---

26   This is hard to track precisely for many reasons, but a figure of about 1 in 100 seems to be widely accepted. The National Institute of Mental Health reported in 2007 that it was found to be 0.6%: http://www.nimh.nih.gov/news/science-news/2007/national-survey-tracks-prevalence-of-personality-disorders-in-us-population.shtml

decriminalized, there is no sensible defense of the huge amount of cost involved with imprisoning millions of people.

There is a clear explicit cost to imprisonment; it's estimated at about $30,000 to $31,000 a year for inmates in the Federal prison system[27].

There is also the tremendous implicit toll that mass incarceration takes on our economy and our communities. Like it or not, when going to prison becomes a normalized behavior, then the rough edges that come with it all become part of a package deal. Those rough edges can become serious: Radicalization, gang membership, recidivism. When we as a society become careless about how we deal with criminals, we pay the consequences later on.

That adds up to a terrible use of our tax dollars and an inexcusable waste of our nation's human capital. **Free people should make free choices and suffer the consequences of their actions.** As a civilization, we should set only as many rules as we actually need to keep ourselves safe, then we need to enforce those rules fairly and equitably, do our best to actually correct the behavior of people who make bad decisions (it's not really a "correctional" system if we're not seriously trying to reform most of our convicts), and keep the truly sociopathic criminals far away from innocent people whom they could harm. It hurts our case if we criminalize too many behaviors.

Contrary to what has been said on the stump, real advocates for law and order should reject a man who openly calls for vigilantism, who threatens unconstitutional actions and behavior, and who would undoubtedly behave in a way that would make Richard Nixon blush if given control of institutions like the FBI.

We have seen enough misbehavior already with the IRS appearing to target conservative groups for special scrutiny. We will not do any good to restore the rule of law if we put those same powers in the hands of an

---

27   Federal Register, "Annual Determination of Average Cost of Incarceration": https://www.federalregister.gov/articles/2015/03/09/2015-05437/annual-determination-of-average-cost-of-incarceration

individual who openly celebrates the use of strong-arm tactics, as Trump does.

It may seem paradoxical, but the real advocates for law and order in 2016 are Gary Johnson and William Weld. **They have earned credibility as the chief executives of two different states, each for two full terms.** They are not proposing any outlandish or extreme new responsibilities or endeavors for the law-enforcement system. What they have advocated is intended as a means to take some pressure off of our overwhelmed prison system, by decriminalizing at the Federal level some behavior that is already widely decriminalized by individual states.

Perhaps above all, neither of them has been dogged by ethics complaints or investigations, and neither has earned any kind of reputation for being on the wrong side of the law. If you want law and order, your best bet is with Johnson and Weld.

Foreign Relations:
A Stable, Responsible America

Every President in the modern era seems to have a foreign-policy "doctrine". The Bush Doctrine openly favored intervention in foreign affairs when that could be seen to favor American values[28], while there is a vigorous debate about what the Obama Doctrine really is[29] – some might argue that it is best defined by the ways it is the opposite of the Bush Doctrine.

In the long run, American foreign policy should acknowledge a seemingly simple but important core truth: **We will have a safe world only when our values are voluntarily adopted worldwide**. What we do to promote, protect, and preserve those values doesn't happen in a vacuum – it often creates feedback loops, both positive and negative.

Regrettably, discussion that should be taking place in this election cycle about our role in the world is largely being overshadowed by the most extreme and extraordinary things being espoused by just one candidate, Donald Trump. That is a grave loss for America. As one of the leading executors of the Obama Doctrine during her time in the State Department, Hillary Clinton has a great deal to contribute to the debate that should be taking place.

But we have failed to get to that debate because at seemingly every turn, the Trump Doctrine has taken center stage. What is the Trump Doctrine? He says it is "America First"[30], but that isn't the truth. His doctrine, fundamentally, is one of **confusing our friends and lending credence to the wildest claims of our enemies**.

---

28   See, for instance, the National Security Strategy published in September 2002: http://georgewbush-whitehouse.archives.gov/nsc/nss/2002/nss1.html

29   Some have reduced it to an off-color quote that can be courteously re-phrased as "Don't do stupid stuff" – see The Atlantic, "The Obama Doctrine": http://www.theatlantic.com/magazine/archive/2016/04/the-obama-doctrine/471525/

30   And that phrase is loaded with historical significance – it was the slogan of isolationists in the time leading up to World War II. See the CNN article, "Trump's 'America First' Has Ugly Echoes from U.S. History": http://www.cnn.com/2016/04/27/opinions/trump-america-first-ugly-echoes-dunn/

Trump's foreign policy originates from the same narrow mindset that has shaped his reputation in business. He has programmed himself to see the world as nothing more than a web of zero-sum interactions. Everything is a "deal", and every deal contains "winners" and "losers"[31].

This worldview may be suitable to real-estate negotiations, in which just two parties are usually involved (seller and buyer) and in which one is usually out to "win" by buying something for less than it is worth or selling it for more than it is worth. But most of the world – including the world of most commercial transactions as well as the universe of international affairs – is vastly more nuanced than that.

In most business interactions, the objective isn't winning versus losing, but rather finding a "win-win" outcome. Partnerships, including favorable relationships with vendors, suppliers, and customers, are the standard – not zero-sum outcomes.

Similarly, in the relationships among nations, instances of voluntary cooperation and mutual benefit are far more attractive than simple binary win/lose interactions. Wars are won and lost, but trade and migration and mutual defense pacts and international agreements are all driven by what is in the common interest.

What exacerbates this trouble is that Trump has extrapolated a frightening conclusion from his zero-sum worldview. **In simple zero-sum interactions, unpredictability can be a major advantage.**

Suppose you're involved in a high-stakes negotiation to buy or sell an office building. If you view your counterparty as an opponent, and your opponent isn't sure what you are thinking or planning, then you may gain an advantage in your negotiations if you can be thoroughly unpredictable. Go through enough negotiations where you are rewarded for unpredictability, and you may begin to believe that it is a superior strategy, suitable for use in all situations.

---

31   This is no abstract argument. A search of his Twitter account in late August 2016 produces hundreds of instances in which he has tweeted the words "loser" or "winner". He ordinarily uses these words in a highly concrete sense.

But unpredictability is suitable only to zero-sum games. Most of the important decisions in life – and in the White House – are not zero-sum.

Trump's worldview and decision-making system are built entirely on zero-sum thinking. He lacks the capacity for abstract thinking as well as the ability to conceive of cooperative solutions. This is not an armchair-psychology observation; he has a long trail of public statements and behavior, and there is not a shred of evidence to suggest that he can assess any set of circumstances in any framework more sophisticated than "winning" and "losing".

That would be unsettling in anyone's interpersonal relationships: Imagine having a co-worker or neighbor who were similarly incapable of seeing anything outside the framework of a zero-sum game. But it is downright reckless to imagine when it involves the powers of the Presidency.

For all her shortcomings, Hillary Clinton clearly demonstrates a capacity to understand things like cooperation. She did, at the very least, experience classic "horse-trading" deals in the Senate and as Secretary of State. At the very least, she can behave within a framework that is appropriate to international affairs.

But even better is the choice of Gary Johnson, who is positively advocating for a clearly cooperative approach to international affairs. Johnson's approach reflects his experience as an independent business owner and as a former chief executive of a state government with an international border. He has embraced "non-intervention" as a guiding standard for his foreign policy[32].

While some Libertarians are thoroughly pacifistic, Johnson has appealed to a policy more suitable to America's inherent role as the world's sole indisputable superpower. In an interview with the editorial

---

32   Military Times, "Libertarian Hopeful Argues for Smaller Military, Less Foreign Intervention": http://www.militarytimes.com/story/military/election/2016/06/22/libertarian-gary-johnson-presidential-town-hall/86273816/

board of the <u>Los Angeles Times</u>, he stated plainly, **"We need to honor our treaty obligations."**[33] Contrast this with Trump's careless undermining of the NATO alliance[34]. The entire value of an alliance such as NATO derives from the steadfastness of resolve its members maintain to come to the mutual defense of one another. To broach even the idea of backing out on those alliances is feckless and fundamentally undermines the protections they are intended to create.

Moreover, in making a cornerstone of his campaign platform out of attacks on the Mexican government (and/or the Mexican people, depending on how one chooses to interpret his profoundly inexact statements on the matter), Trump has not only neglected the facts, he has made it harder to achieve the kind of cooperation that is in the common interests of both countries. He carelessly bashes immigrants and accuses the Mexican government of all kinds of implied malfeasance, ignoring the real facts – that net migration is actually into Mexico from the United States, rather than the other way around[35], and that the United States has a role to play in reducing the impact of things like cross-border violence tied to the drug trade.

Rather than demonizing immigrants, Gary Johnson has taken the opposite course, saying, "We should be embracing immigration"[36] and standing for a policy of much-needed immigration reform.

Thoughtful, cooperative engagement isn't possible with every country. We're not about to have friendly sit-down sessions with the governments of North Korea or Syria. But as voters, we have to draw the line: It undermines our national security to threaten long-established defense agreements like the NATO pact. It ignores reality to categorically demonize immigrants or to threaten our international

---

33   See the transcript (albeit posted under a strongly anti-Johnson headline) at <u>Los Angeles Times</u>, "Possible Presidential Spoiler Gary Johnson Speaks to The Times Editorial Board About Siphoning Votes from Hillary Clinton": http://www.latimes.com/opinion/editorials/la-ed-gary-johnson-libertarian-transcript-20160729-snap-story.html

34   To be exact, Trump said, "I think NATO is obsolete" to the editorial board of the <u>New York Times</u>: http://www.nytimes.com/2016/03/27/us/politics/donald-trump-transcript.html

35   Pew Research Center, "More Mexicans Leaving Than Coming to the U.S.": http://www.pewhispanic.org/2015/11/19/more-mexicans-leaving-than-coming-to-the-u-s/

36   <u>The Hill</u>, "Gary Johnson: Trump's Mexico Wall 'Asinine'": http://thehill.com/blogs/ballot-box/presidential-races/291742-gary-johnson-trumps-mexico-wall-asinine

neighbors. And it is unacceptable to center our foreign policy under the long-discredited notion of isolationism.

We deserve to know more about what would emerge under a Clinton Doctrine; we have seen a campaign promise that it will include robust national defense and ongoing international engagement[37], but there is reasonable cause for concern that the former chief administrator of the Obama Doctrine may give us more of the same.

We have no evidence of any serious Trump Doctrine, but the preponderance of the evidence suggests that he is temperamentally programmed to see the entire balance of world relations from a dangerously flawed perspective. **The world is not made of zero-sum games**, very few matters in international affairs involve a binary outcome of winner-versus-loser, and unpredictability and antagonism are not useful qualities in the character of a President.

What we can read into a Johnson Doctrine is a projection of strength not just through the possession of a powerful military, but also from cooperative engagement around the world. Non-interventionism is not the same as isolationism or pacifism. We have to continue to believe that the world will be safer when other countries voluntarily adopt the values that we embrace. **Constructive engagement with other countries** – not antagonism – is the way to nurture that outcome.

---

37   Hillary Clinton campaign website: https://www.hillaryclinton.com/issues/national-security/

Promote Productive Capitalism and Restrain Cronyism

Anyone who doubts the productive capacities of capitalism is either blind to – or willfully ignorant of – the tremendous improvement in living standards experienced by ordinary Americans over the course of the 20th Century. There is no alternative economic system that has yet come close to achieving the kind of broad-based improvement in the material quality of life that has been brought about by America's "light-touch" relationship between government and the private sector. **Government can be a valuable supporting player, but the private sector does the heavy lifting in the economy.**

Government has a role to play in the economy. That isn't in serious dispute. But the role is a supporting one: The government is needed to referee certain forms of exchange to keep different parties from hurting one another, and it can serve a useful role in regulating certain monopolistic industries and in supplying some essential services, like the Interstate highway system.

However, when government takes too expansive a role in the economy – even when it does so under the cover of trying to do things like "helping the middle class" – it runs a very high risk of disrupting the markets that would have otherwise found efficient ways to do the same things.

Even worse, regulations and other government interventions often end up harming ordinary consumers and creating benefits only for those who have political access or influence. This is a problem that is easy to miss, because it requires looking below the surface: The more the government is empowered to control the economy, the more incentive there is to manipulate government officials, through both legal and illegal means. **When government has lots of economic power, the people who have power within government have something very valuable to sell.**

Understanding the intrinsic value of political power is critical to understanding the threat posed by an over-active government role in the economy.

Hillary Clinton has been pushed to the left by the long nomination contest against Bernie Sanders. To appease a leftward-tilting Democratic base, she will have to run on a platform of bigger government – a government that expands entitlements like free college tuition[38]. These promises are profoundly expensive.

Even if she is really a pro-business Democrat at heart (like Bill Clinton was), that wing of her party has literally disbanded: The Democratic Leadership Council, or DLC, doesn't exist anymore. The DLC was, in effect, the home of centrist "Third Way" policies within the Democratic Party – ideas like balanced budgets and free trade. It fell apart in 2011[39] and hasn't been replaced. It simply lost too much ground to the much more activist "progressive" wing of the party, particularly with the rise and reelection of President Barack Obama. **Without a defined pro-market caucus within the Democratic Party, Hillary Clinton has no reason to appeal to it.** Whether she is or is not a pro-business politician at heart, her party has moved far in the opposite direction.

Donald Trump stands unashamedly in favor of cronyism in politics, business, and government. He doesn't speak of smaller government because he doesn't understand it nor does he care about it. **Trump's form of populism is about expanding the role of government**, even as he decries the people who run it today. His attacks are on the personnel, not the system. He openly embraces the manipulation of the political system to achieve ends that enrich him, from his enthusiastic use of bankruptcy laws to the favors he claims to have called in from politicians in exchange for campaign contributions.

Furthermore, in Trump's view of economics (such as it is), the United States needs to erect giant barriers to international trade, like a 45% tax

---

38 Her campaign website specifically promises a program to ensure that "Every student should have the option to graduate from a public college or university in their state without taking on any student debt": https://www.hillaryclinton.com/issues/college/

39 Politico, "The End of the DLC Era": http://www.politico.com/story/2011/02/the-end-of-the-dlc-era-049041

on goods imported from China[40]. He takes a stand on outsourcing that sounds downright authoritarian, saying, "And if companies want to leave Arizona and if they want to leave other states, there's going to be a lot of trouble for them. It's not going to be so easy. There will be consequence [sic]. Remember that. There will be consequence [sic]."[41] **In stark contrast to the idea of free markets operating under the rule of law, Trump threatens profoundly restricted markets operating under the rule of his temper.**

He also adopts a view of international trade that threatens to upend every standing trade agreement we have. Hearkening back to his zero-sum vision of the world, Trump talks as though the United States has somehow been backed into a corner by wily negotiators from every other part of the world and cowed into submission[42]. The idea is ludicrous.

On the whole, the United States benefits mightily from international trade, both explicitly and implicitly. We benefit from access to foreign markets for the many things we produce in great surplus – from agricultural commodities to aircraft. The United States has massive economic advantages in the production of many outputs, and it is a cornerstone of economic behavior that we ought to do as much as we can of those things at which we have the greatest advantages.

Implicitly, we benefit as well. Nations that trade with one another rarely go to war. Just as with exchange taking place between individuals, we don't have to agree in order to trade – but trade tends to make it easier to get along. And as trade helps countries become more prosperous, that rising prosperity tends to help discourage bloodlust. Who wants to go to war when there are profits to be made?

---

40   New York Times, "Donald Trump Says He Favors Big Tariffs on Chinese Exports":
     http://www.nytimes.com/politics/first-draft/2016/01/07/donald-trump-says-he-favors-big-tariffs-on-chinese-exports/
41   From the New York Times transcript of his speech on August 31, 2016:
     http://www.nytimes.com/2016/09/02/us/politics/transcript-trump-immigration-speech.html
42   Again from the New York Times transcript of his August 31, 2016 speech ("We're going to renegotiate trade deals [...] We have the most incompetently worked trade deals ever negotiated probably in the history of the world"):
     http://www.nytimes.com/2016/09/02/us/politics/transcript-trump-immigration-speech.html

Again, this does not suggest that trade is perfect or that it comes without consequences. Some people are and will be hurt by trade, especially if they happen to be employed in sectors where their countries lose competitive advantages over others. This effect takes place within countries, too: Long before the American textile industry lost most of its ground to other countries, the North lost most of its textile production to the South. Some widely-known companies that started as makers of fabrics (including Berkshire Hathaway and Textron) remain in business today, having long ago abandoned the textile industry and adapted to compete in more favorable markets.

It is inevitable that trade and technology will both cause some businesses and industries to lose ground. That much is unavoidable. What matters is whether the firms and workers affected are able to adapt, and whether the economy as a whole can grow through new innovation and other adjustments and emerge stronger and more robust in the end.

Both of these visions of government and the economy – Clinton's ever-expanding entitlements and Trump's extraordinary threats to shut down our trade system – are at odds with what is best for Americans.

Yet there is an even larger hazard looming: **We are running out of time to rein in the Federal debt.** The longer we wait, the greater the pain. Donald Trump has already revealed the sliver of a plan he has in mind: He thinks the United States can simply inflate the currency right out of budget trouble[43]. In theory, any country that controls its own currency can do that.

But Trump's positively outlandish proposal overlooks several unavoidable factors and extraordinary consequences that could follow from his wildly misguided threat:

■ The Federal Reserve is independent of the government (as it must be for the security of the currency, for exactly a threat like

---

43   CNN, "Why Donald Trump's Debt Proposal is Reckless": http://money.cnn.com/2016/05/09/news/economy/donald-trump-us-debt/

this). Governments that inflate their way out of debt have no reason to impose fiscal discipline, so they don't.

- Inflation kills savings, which ultimately kills an economy and inescapably punishes those who have been responsible by saving for themselves.
- The strength of the U.S. economy relies in part upon the reliability of our currency – it is the reserve currency of the world. An inflationary approach to erasing our debt would instantly destroy the credibility of the dollar in world exchange, leading to devastating economic consequences. It's so dangerous a threat that even speaking it aloud is enough to set the world's traders and investors on edge. **It is much too serious a hazard to even joke about.** But once Trump puts it on the table as a possibility, he invites people who do not understand the consequences to side with his nuclear option.

While Hillary Clinton does not seem to have adopted a similar outlandish vision for dealing with the Federal debt, her expensive laundry list of proposals for new spending only guarantees that the government would end up as broke as ever.

In sharp contrast to these two deeply broken visions of government and economics stands the Johnson-Weld ticket's view of the appropriate role for government. As governors, Gary Johnson and William Weld earned applause for fiscal responsibility. (Note, by the way, that as a former governor, Johnson has experience with negotiating a budget with a legislature that neither Donald Trump nor Hillary Clinton can similarly claim.)

Gary Johnson deserves substantial credit for acknowledging the important reality that government can't honestly take credit for "creating" jobs; even the very language of his campaign website acknowledges that government's role is to create an environment in which the private sector can perform job creation[44].

---

44   JohnsonWeld.com: https://www.johnsonweld.com/jobs

And even more crucially, **the Johnson-Weld platform places a balanced budget at the top of its list of priorities**[45]. The consequences of over-spending grow more perilous with every passing day. Like a person engaged in reckless behavior (like speeding without wearing a seat belt or smoking two packs of cigarettes a day), the Federal government's spending policies put us at grave and well-known risk. We don't know exactly when we might face a serious moment of reckoning, but we do know that our path is extremely hazardous and is bound to end in disaster if we do not change. **When only one campaign acknowledges a serious – perhaps even existential – risk, that campaign must be taken seriously by responsible voters.** Failing to take the issue or the campaign seriously gives the other campaigns carte blanche to take the country's attention away from the important and to focus it on the trivial – or worse.

---

45   This is meant literally: The section devoted to balancing the Federal budget is the first item in the list of all campaign issues displayed at https://www.johnsonweld.com/issues

A side note on business experience

Historically, one of the paths to success in earning a Republican nomination has included at least some direct experience as a businessperson. Mitt Romney, George W. Bush, and George H. W. Bush[46] each had significant private-sector experience in addition to their government experience prior to being nominated for President.

Hillary Clinton has no significant business experience, other than her past as an attorney in private practice. But Donald Trump's experience isn't in constructive work, either. He has been a real-estate trader his entire career. And while he has shown a gift for marketing and self-promotion, his words and deeds alike project the psychology of a man who doesn't understand the nature of productive business.

Real estate trading is inherently speculative in nature: Like oil, gold, or collectible coins, the buyer hopes to find someone in the future who is willing to pay an even higher price. A property owner may collect rents, of course, but even the value of rent is subject to massive fluctuations far beyond the owner's control[47]. Every market is subject to change, competition, and uncertainty – but in most sectors, real and measurable value can be created by the producer. A dentist can hire new hygienists and attend classes for continuing education. A farmer can adjust rates of fertilizer and pesticide application to optimize crop production (even if the weather can be unpredictable). A factory production manager can modernize equipment and retrain workers to increase the number of widgets produced per hour.

Donald Trump, by contrast, employs his own name and reputation as his primary means of increasing the value of his holdings. Remember that he owns some properties, has a leveraged interest in others, and strictly licenses his name to others. This is why he says his net worth

---

46   It's often overlooked in his biography, but George H. W. Bush was a successful oil man before he entered politics. See the PBS biography at http://www.pbs.org/wgbh/americanexperience/features/biography/bush-george/

47   Perhaps nowhere is this more true than in Manhattan. See the wild swings documented by Green Street Advisors at http://www.greenstreetadvisors.com/pdf/press/moppi/GSAMOPI.pdf

depends upon how he feels from day to day[48]. While there is nothing illegal or immoral about it, a business that is subject to whims of such a nature is not operating in the same productive sphere as a dental practice, a farm, or a factory. Trump operates in a very universe far removed from the normal circumstances of productive capitalism, and it is one in which he is rewarded for bluster.

Trump's gift for self-promotion makes him a lot like Kanye West. Both of them have a particular genius for one very narrow thing that makes them look bigger than they really are. Just like Kanye West is a savant for lyrics, Donald Trump is a savant for self-promotion. But that doesn't make either of them a genius at anything else.

Gary Johnson's experience as a business owner began in college, and it was literally constructive from the start: He began as a construction contractor. His understanding of the world of business isn't that of a man who got his start in the world of Manhattan real estate trading with his father's backing – it's that of a man who paid his way through college by starting and expanding a small business, and who subsequently grew it organically into a major construction firm[49].

A person can be a qualified and reasonable candidate for office without having worked in the private sector. But Donald Trump touts his private-sector experience as his sole qualification for office, has no prior experience whatsoever as an elected executive, and refuses to release his tax records so that his extraordinary claims to wealth and success can be subjected to actual scrutiny[50]. This means he should be held to a high standard to prove (a) that he understands the full spectrum of American business beyond real estate (he has not); (b) that he grasps the differences between the roles of a businessperson with the

---

48   CNN, "Trump: I'm Worth Whatever I Feel":
      http://money.cnn.com/2011/04/21/news/companies/donald_trump/
49   See an Associated Press report published by the Amarillo Globe-News, "Gov. Johnson Sells
      Big J Enterprises":
      http://amarillo.com/stories/1999/08/29/new_LG3542.002.shtml#.V8udZpgrLIU
50   Note that the only Trump tax records that have become public are profoundly unflattering.
      See Washington Post, "Trump Once Revealed His Income Tax Returns. They Showed He
      Didn't Pay a Cent.": https://www.washingtonpost.com/politics/trumps-income-tax-returns-
      once-became-public-they-showed-he-didnt-pay-a-cent/2016/05/20/ffa2f63c-1b7c-11e6-b6e0-
      c53b7ef63b45_story.html

proverbial name on the door and that of an elected official (again, he has not); and, (c) that he is in fact a measurable success and not just an extraordinary braggart (he has not done this, either).

Gary Johnson can point to his very public record as a two-term governor, but he can also point to his business success as confirmation of his beliefs: Johnson wants limited government for the same reasons as any other business owner – because he has literally experienced the life of an entrepreneur first-hand. That was his formative experience.

If anyone is to be considered a credible candidate by people who resist the enlargement of government at the expense of the private sector, it ought to be the one who can take pride in building a significant company from scratch and then putting his principles to work while in office – not the one who takes pride in exploiting tax loopholes[51] and influence-peddling while refusing to release records indicating that he pays any Federal tax at all. **Gary Johnson has bona fide credentials as a small-government, pro-market businessperson and as a public official who acted upon those principles.** Donald Trump does not.

---

51 One cannot fully understand Donald Trump's real-estate work without studying his first major "deal" – the conversion of Manhattan's Commodore Hotel into the Grand Hyatt. Much of the story has disappeared from contemporary memory because it went down before the Internet Age, but the Los Angeles Times has digitally published a 1994 article entitled "Hyatt Owners Sue Trump for $100 Million" that tells the reader enough: http://articles.latimes.com/1994-03-29/business/fi-39687_1_grand-hyatt

Social Conservatives Should Advocate Limited Government

As a philosophy, libertarianism is often distilled down to "fiscally conservative and socially liberal". That may not instinctively sit well with people who consider themselves social conservatives.

Hillary Clinton may not be socially conservative, but Donald Trump is even worse – he poses as a social conservative exclusively as a matter of convenience. He's happy to accept endorsements from religious leaders, but it's evident that he has no strong moral bearing, religious or otherwise. Expediency alone is what satisfies him.

It is much worse to worship a false prophet than to remain a skeptic of it all.

Social issues often find themselves adjudicated in the public square, whether by courts or by popular vote, but in the end, all cultural matters are resolved within individual hearts and minds. Of the three choices certain to be on the ballot in November, the one likely to do the least objective harm to a socially conservative worldview is the libertarian choice – the one that says government ought to remain out of matters of personal choice and conscience. Gary Johnson and William Weld have referred to their philosophy as "fiscally conservative and socially tolerant" – a slight adaptation of the more common description of libertarianism. And the very simple reality is this: Johnson and Weld acknowledge that there are extremely important and urgent issues that face the next administration – like taking immediate action to rein in the Federal debt. If they are to be believed (and if their records as governors are any indication), **their efforts will be focused primarily on rolling back the reach and cost of government**. While that will not affirmatively promote a socially conservative agenda, it ought to leave many issues to be decided by hearts and minds – not by government activism.

"Tolerance" is a powerful word. To be tolerant is to accept that opinions will differ, often on important issues. And tolerance is exactly what the Founders of this nation had in mind.

Thomas Jefferson insisted that just three things appear on his epitaph:

> "[T]he following inscription, & not a word more: Here was buried Thomas Jefferson[,] Author of the Declaration of American Independence[,] of the Statute of Virginia for religious freedom[,] & Father of the University of Virginia[52]"

That Statute for Religious Freedom, which Jefferson thought was one of his three greatest contributions to the world, centers on the following line:

"[T]he opinions of men are not the object of civil government, nor under its jurisdiction"[53]

Mutual toleration is the only practice that is compatible with the beliefs of the Founders.

Besides, what is peddled by the Trump campaign is scarcely even a shadow of conservatism. It is not socially conservative for Donald Trump to threaten religious institutions like mosques on the premise of fighting terrorism[54] – in fact, it is quite the opposite.

Since the founding days of the republic, when Pennsylvania was a Quaker state, Maryland a Catholic colony, and Massachusetts the home of the Puritans, it has been understood that **a threat to any religion is a threat to all** – even if we haven't always been successful at putting this belief into action. That includes unpopular religions – in the past, those have include Judaism, Mormonism, and Roman Catholicism, among others. To threaten a ban on the entry of Muslims

---

52   Thomas Jefferson Foundation, "Jefferson's Gravestone": https://www.monticello.org/site/research-and-collections/jeffersons-gravestone
53   National Archives, Jefferson Papers: http://founders.archives.gov/documents/Jefferson/01-02-02-0132-0004-0082
54   CNN, "Trump Doubles Down on Calls for Mosque Surveillance": http://www.cnn.com/2016/06/15/politics/donald-trump-muslims-mosque-surveillance/

into the United States, as Trump has done[55], is simply to re-cast old prejudices against a new target. Matters of religion and personal belief should not be subject to political control. The only legitimate political role in these matters is to keep one person from harming another.

The Republican Party has been harmed on an electoral basis for straying from this belief. The truly conservative stand is one of non-interference between faith and politics. Donald Trump's exploitation of faithful people as tools of his own political enlargement is not socially conservative.

For the voter who sincerely holds conservative social beliefs, the credible option is that of the ticket that promises non-interference with individual conscience – and in 2016, that is the Libertarian ticket.

---

55   Washington Post, "Donald Trump is Expanding his Muslim Ban, Not Rolling It Back": https://www.washingtonpost.com/news/post-politics/wp/2016/07/24/donald-trump-is-expanding-his-muslim-ban-not-rolling-it-back/

The Honorable Alternative

The Best Caretaker is the One Who Promises to Do the Least

US Senator Ben Sasse of Nebraska, a disaffected Republican, put it well when he suggested that the United States may need a "caretaker" President[56] for a term (or two), while the nation takes some time to reassess where it is headed in the long run.

Sen. Sasse's plea for a caretaker President highlights the need to address a handful of urgent issues facing the country, with no sweeping ambitions to accomplish other revolutionary change. Starting with Sasse's list (adapted and expanded below), one could easily identify several urgent issues that could easily take up every second of a four-year term to get under control:

- The ballooning Federal debt (not to mention the extensive unfunded obligations building within our Federal entitlement programs that exceed the existing debt already on the books).

- The 21st Century threats of cyber, nuclear, biological, and chemical warfare (including asymmetric warfare – better known as terrorism).

- The worrisome state of the national infrastructure – visible in everything from the collapse of the I-35W bridge in the Twin Cities to the lead emergency in the water supply of Flint, Michigan.

Not to belabor the question, but who would be better suited to addressing the most urgent problems facing government than someone with a demonstrated philosophy of limited government? The person who believes in strictly limiting government has the strongest credentials of all when it comes to expecting that government do its job well.

---

56   The Senator shared this in a Facebook post entitled, "An Open Letter to Majority America": https://www.facebook.com/sassefornebraska/posts/593031420862025

The more specific the objectives, the more accountable the outcomes. Nobody expects much from a restaurant buffet promising a hundred different choices – that's simply too many things for all (or even many) of them to be done well. But by contrast, many communities hold "restaurant weeks" during which participating establishments offer a simplified prix-fixe menu, showcasing the best of what they offer. The patron who orders something off a restaurant-week menu can reasonably expect that what is served will be the best the establishment has to offer. No restauranteur is going to promote his or her fifth-best dish during restaurant week. **Fewer promises, backed by a serious record of delivering on past promises, mean greater accountability for executing on the things that matter.**

People who think government can and should do everything have little accountability – real accountability comes from the people who expect government to do a limited number of things and to do those things well.

Thus, the ideal "caretaker" in a time of urgent need is the one with the most limited ambitions for getting government to do more. Of the three candidates who are assured to be on the ballots in all 50 states in November, Hillary Clinton is no small-government crusader, Donald Trump has explicitly favored larger government, and **Gary Johnson has a documented track record of achieving smaller government**.

If anything resembling a modern conservative philosophy is to survive in the years ahead, its proponents must choose a narrow focus: Budgetary responsibility, a real focus on security (not symbolic nonsense backed only with bluster), and freedom. These only stand a chance if people are steadfast about voting for them. And if you don't vote for them in 2016, you can be almost certain they won't be on the ballot in 2020 – and by then the damage will only be compounded by our inaction.

We can't afford to waste decades waiting for conservatism to come around again. The political life cycle rewards big government for decades at a time before people finally wake up and roll it back. The era of Reagan and Thatcher was a rollback period. Irreparable harm will be done to the philosophy of limited government if we don't draw a clear distinction in November 2016 between big and small government. Donald Trump won't do that, because he fundamentally does not understand nor care about a philosophy of government. If you wish to send a message rejecting the big-government worldview ascendant within the Democratic Party, you must also clearly reject Trump's ego-driven goulash of a platform. The honorable alternative is to cast a vote with the limited-government ticket of Johnson and Weld.

The Honorable Alternative

Send a Message in 2016

There is much to frustrate the reasonable voter in 2016. The two major parties have selected nominees who are in a unique competition not so much to win over the electorate as to make the other look even more unpalatable.

If Hillary Clinton thinks she is above the law[57], then Donald Trump doesn't even have the capacity to realize that the law exists.

To cite just two examples:

- He has threatened to "open up libel laws", which fundamentally undermines the entire notion of a free press in America[58]

- He told members of the House of Representatives that he would defend "Article XII" of the Constitution, when no such article exists. He is so flippant about the rule of law that in a meeting intended to reassure elected Republicans that he would be a responsible President, he managed to make it clear he lacks even a basic understanding of the Constitution.[59]

The Presidency isn't a reward for a popularity contest. It is a solemn duty that involves matters as grave as life and death, often for many, and far more frequently than mortals should be expected to encounter such questions. It is – without question – not a job suited to someone so inarticulate, so obtuse, and so reckless with the facts that he doesn't understand the document that originated the job in the first place.

To be clear about his shortcomings:

---

57 As evidenced, just for instance, by the extraordinary carelessness and pathological evasion that surround the use (and later destruction) of a private e-mail system while in office as Secretary of State

58 CNN, "Donald Trump Wants to 'Open Up' Libel Laws So He Can Sue Press": http://money.cnn.com/2016/02/26/media/donald-trump-libel-laws/

59 Wall Street Journal, "Donald Trump's Pledge to Defend Article XII of Constitution Raises Eyebrows": http://blogs.wsj.com/washwire/2016/07/07/donald-trumps-pledge-to-defend-article-xii-of-constitution-raises-eyebrows/

- Donald Trump has a disqualifying lack of curiosity about the world. Despite months of criticism, he has not given a single shred of evidence that he is seeking to enlighten himself before (potentially) assuming the role of President.

- Donald Trump is possessed of a deficit of character so toxic, so irredeemable, and so fundamental that it cannot be salvaged. He didn't know enough to reject the poster boy for white supremacy in America – even when clearly challenged on the issue and given multiple opportunities to rescind his error. He openly mocked the service of POWs including Sen. John McCain.

- Donald Trump defaults to mockery, insults, and petty name-calling publicly and at every turn, resisting not only the decency to think twice before engaging with people like an undisciplined toddler, but also refusing to recant or correct his errors even when called out in the most public of forums.

The presidency calls for temperament, judgment, capacity, and experience. Donald Trump has none of those. Hillary Clinton has meaningful shortcomings (as well as a laundry list of bad policy ideas), but at least rises to levels of basic competence. Gary Johnson, by contrast with both, is a refreshing and credible alternative.

The 2016 election is an opportunity to be on the right side of history, particularly for people who are normally right of center on the political spectrum.

Trumpism acts like hydrogen sulfide: In small doses, hydrogen sulfide is what gives sewer gas its obnoxious odor. In larger doses, people become numb to the scent, and over time, exposure to high doses becomes lethal.

Similarly, Trumpism in small doses is obnoxious – but as its dosage is increased, we become numb to its effects. Each new outrageous claim or willfully ignorant or offensive statement simply crowds out the one that came the day before. And in time, the high dose becomes lethal to civil behavior.

That's why we've seen violence at his rallies and can expect a general corrosion of civility as he remains in the public eye. The FCC several years ago was forced to rule that "fleeting expletives" were no longer strictly forbidden – because the sitting Vice President, Dick Cheney, was caught using salty language on an open microphone, the courts decided that civilians couldn't be prosecuted for uttering the same words in the same manner on broadcast airwaves[60].

If you think it was a step in the wrong direction culturally for the Vice President to use a naughty word or two near a microphone, then heaven help us should the occupant of the Oval Office become a man whose overt racism, sexism, and thuggery are unrestricted by any bounds of common sense or decency. Trumpism is a virus that has infected the Republican Party, and it may be fatal to the party. Whatever one might think of the two major parties, our system of voting will tend to produce two major parties as the stable outcome. When one of those parties becomes dangerously unstable, it risks undermining the legitimacy of the process itself.

The Trump campaign is destined for catastrophe, most likely in both the immediate and longer-term futures. If you don't believe that, you don't understand demographics.

What Trumpism is doing will set back the limited-government agenda for a generation. Left-wing, big-government policies will become normalized among an entire generation of young voters (particularly those under age 35). They will see the Republican Party as the home of cranky old white men, and that will lead to the permanent isolation of a limited-government agenda.

The only way to fight back is to register a protest vote. Third-party campaigns are usually destined for failure; a two-party system is the only stable outcome of a first-past-the-post electoral system. But the

---

60 Chicago Tribune, "Bad Words and the FCC", http://articles.chicagotribune.com/2007-06-09/news/0706080740_1_indecency-ruling-obscenity-rules-then-fcc-chairman-michael-powell

current system isn't stable; the coalitions that make up the two parties have spun wildly out of control, and a re-alignment is now inevitable. **The only way to ensure that the limited-government side gets a hearing is to register a clear protest vote against Trumpism.**

We have to say, "I am here, and I will not roll over for the Big Government of the left or of the right." Your vote will not be counted if you abstain (either by staying home on Election Day or by leaving the top of your ballot unmarked), and it won't measure for anything if you vote for Trump. If you truly object to the expanse of government, you have to register an affirmative vote for an alternative.

No, this isn't "throwing away your vote". This is an extraordinary election. If you don't register a protest this time, the fiscally conservative, socially tolerant wing of the Republican Party (and of the nation itself) will be disorganized and likely without an organizing structure or voice by the 2020 election.

Stand on principle and reject the virus. You do not have to like Hillary Clinton, and you may have substantial reason to register a vote in opposition to her philosophy or her practices. But the shortcomings of Donald Trump far outweigh any benefit to be gained by protesting against Clinton.

In 2016, it is possible to vote in a nasty, awful election, and to do so with honor. **The honorable alternative** to the Democratic and Republican choices is to vote for **the highly qualified, unquestionably experienced, and philosophically sound duo of Gary Johnson for President and William Weld for Vice President.**

A Final Word

Calling one campaign the "honorable" alternative to the others doesn't mean that it is right about everything. As it has been said before, if you want to vote for a candidate who agrees with you 100%, you'll have to write in yourself.

But the Presidency should be an office of trust, decency, and dignity. It should also be one that respects its Constitutional bounds. We shouldn't look to the President to initiate policy – we should look to the President to faithfully execute the laws passed by Congress, and to serve as a check on bad policies of government overreach and other error. Remember, the Constitution gives the President the power to veto bills, not to initiate them[61].

That restraint is the essence of the fiscally conservative, socially tolerant message of the campaign of Gary Johnson and William Weld. They don't have to be perfect to be able to do the job with honor. They are human beings, and humans will make mistakes. But their records suggest that those errors will be ones of fact or even judgment – but not of basic decency or character.

America deserves leadership with honor and with the humility to show restraint in the use of power. We deserve the honorable alternative of Gary Johnson and Bill Weld.

---

61   Get to know Article I, Section 7 of the Constitution:
http://www.archives.gov/exhibits/charters/constitution_transcript.html